Zen Comma

David Bowman

Zen Comma

by David Bowman

Write Well Publishing

ISBN: 978-0-9885078-4-5

Published by Write Well Publishing
Printed in the United States of America

TABLE OF CONTENTS

INTRODUCTION

Do commas confuse you?

The final stage of the writing process is proofreading: correcting any errors in spelling, punctuation, word usage, and format. Roughly 75% of what I do while proofreading clients' documents is correct commas.

When I teach community writing courses at the university, I ask the students, "What's the number one thing that confuses you about punctuation and grammar?" In every class, someone says "Commas," and about half of the students nod in agreement.

Commas confuse most people. Unlike other types of punctuation, they are used in so many ways. The purpose of this book is to show you how to use them correctly.

If you want to write clearly and professionally, you need to use commas correctly.

Why Zen Is Part of the Book Name

This is, obviously, not a book on Zen. This is a book on commas. However, core Zen principles provide the framework for understanding and using commas to achieve clear communication.

Zen emphasizes experiential understanding gained through meditating (focused, purposeful consideration) and practicing a right way of living. This is not so different to how we learn, say, commas.

We study the comma rules, think about them and how they are used, seek to understand their underlying concepts, and put them into practice. Zen is anti-theoretical in nature, and commas, too, are practical tools that we use to accomplish communication goals.

"Don't expect your practice to be clear of obstacles. Without hindrances, the mind that seeks enlightenment may be burnt out" –Zen Master Kyong Ho. However, as one Zen proverb states, "From the withered tree, a flower blooms."

The purpose of Zen, if it can be said to have a single purpose, is awakening. Similarly, commas awaken, or reveal, the meanings in our sentences. They reveal what we are trying to say, and they are necessary to communicate that message to our readers.

Commas are Zen.

Chapter Organization

Each chapter begins with correct examples, explains the rules for correct usage, covers common errors, and discusses special considerations so you can use commas correctly, intelligently, and conscientiously.

The various koans interspersed throughout the chapters are intended to help you "meditate" on comma concepts. When you understand these koans, you will be able to apply their concepts to your own writing.

The following sample chapter describes what you will find in each chapter of Zen Comma.

Sample Chapter Structure

0.   Chapter Number and Title, A Basic Use of the Comma

0.1.   CORRECT SAMPLE of this type of comma use so you can see how it's used correctly.

0.2.   Another CORRECT SAMPLE of this type of comma use

RULE 0
The comma rule discussed in the immediately following section

Information about how to use the comma correctly: Instructions, considerations, and explanations of the correct samples above.

Possibly confusing term. An explanation of a possibly confusing term. Sometimes, we need to use new terms to explain the comma usage. This section helps you understand the term so that you can understand the explanation of the comma use.

0.3.   A wrong sample, designated by an asterisk.*

More information about this type of comma use.

0.4.   Another correct sample, usually based on some special consideration.

More information about this type of use, common mistakes, and things to remember.

Koan #

A short anecdote about Bumbo as he learns to use commas correctly. Reflecting on these anecdotes will help you grasp the underlying concepts of comma use. Explanations of the koans are in the back of the book.

What Do Commas Do?

Commas are visual clues that have only one purpose: Help the reader separate parts of sentences into discrete, meaningful messages.

A sentence may have multiple parts. Each part has some meaning that we are trying to communicate. We combine those parts to write a sentence that has a single message. In most cases, we identify those parts by separating them with commas. This helps the reader find them and understand the overall message of the sentence.

And that, ultimately, is why we use commas: Help the readers understand the ideas we want to communicate.

Do commas matter? Yes!

As you will see throughout this book, where we put the commas, and where we leave them out, can **change the meaning of a sentence**.

When we're writing, we already know what we want to say. The reader doesn't. Our job, therefore, is to help the reader understand our meaning.

And that means the commas have to be right.

1. Commas in Series

1.1. The toy was red, round, and heavy.

1.2. I purchased pickles at the store, gas at the convenience store, and flowers at the florist for my beautiful wife.

RULE A
Separate every item in a series with a comma.

Series. A *series* is a string of three or more matching items in a sentence. For example, the series in sample 1.1 contains three items: *red, round,* and *heavy.* The series in sample 1.2 also contains three items.

Take a look at sample 1.1 and see how the commas fit the rule. The first item is *red,* and it is separated from *round* by a comma. The second item is *round,* and it is separated from *red* and *heavy* by commas. Every item in the series is separated from the other items by commas.

1.3. I respect my parents, Fred and Gloria.

1.4. I respect my parents, the president and the first lady.*

1.5. I respect my parents, the president, and the first lady.

Samples 1.3–1.5 help to understand why we use a comma before the final *and, but,* or *or.* Let's look at them carefully and see what they might mean to the reader.

In sample 1.3, the reader will most likely interpret this sentence to mean "I respect my parents," and the names of my parents are *Fred* and *Gloria.* The reader might think I respect my parents, I respect another person named *Fred,* and I respect yet another person named *Gloria,* but this is unlikely.

The most likely interpretation is that *Fred* and *Gloria*

are the names of my parents. The sentence structure and comma use lead the reader to that conclusion. (We'll see more about this type of comma use in the section on Commas with Appositives.)

Now look at sample 1.4. This has the same sentence structure and comma use as sample 1.3. How will the reader interpret this sentence? Well, the reader could interpret this to mean my parents are the president and the first lady, which is not true. We need the final comma used in sample 1.5 to make clear that we're talking about 3 groups of people: (1) my parents, (2) the president, and (3) the first lady. This leads us to our next rule.

RULE B
Use the serial comma.

The comma before *and*, *but*, or *or* that introduces the final item is called the *serial comma*. It is also called the *Harvard comma* and the *Oxford comma*.

The Associated Press (AP) style guide, which governs most journalism writing, tells writers not to use the serial comma. This may be an attempt to save a little column space for words by removing punctuation. Nearly every other style guide says to use it—and for a good reason.

As we see from samples 1.3–1.5, the serial comma, or its absence, can affect how the reader interprets the sentence. When we leave it out, we increase the possibility that the reader will misunderstand the sentence. When we leave it in, we clearly identify each item in the series.

Here's another example of how that comma makes a difference.

1.6.   Susan, Fritz and Tom and Julie have one dog each.*

How many dogs are we talking about in sample 1.6? Possible answers are 2, 3, and 4. If we put the comma after *Tom*, we know the sentence describes 3 dogs.

1.7.   Susan, Fritz and Tom, and Julie have one dog each.

The serial comma in sample 1.7 tells the reader that Susan has 1 dog, Fritz and Tom have 1 dog together, and Julie has 1 dog. The comma is required to make this clear to the reader.

But what if the parts are obvious, such as in sample 1.1? Do we still need the serial comma?

Remember, the purpose of the comma is to help the reader find the meaningful parts in a sentence. Although we could remove it sometimes without confusing the reader, other times it is necessary to make our meaning clear. That brings us to a general principle for commas (and all punctuation):

What we do sometimes for clarity, we do all the time for consistency.

Using the serial comma is never going to be wrong (unless you are required to use the AP style guide), so be consistent.

While we're on the topic of series, I'll make another point to help you separate items in series.

RULE C
Use semicolons to separate items that have their own commas.

Sometimes, the items may be complex, meaning they have their own commas. If any of the items have commas, use semi-colons to separate them, as follows.

1.8.   This is my brother, Bob; his friend; and my wife.

Even if only one of the items has its own commas, as in sample 1.8, separate every item with a semicolon.

Some word processors have an option to require the serial comma when checking grammar and spelling. I recommend you turn it on.

Koan 1

Bumbo approached his teacher and said, "Teacher, I was taught not to use the comma before the word 'and.' Is that true?"

The teacher asked in return, "When did you become a journalist?"

Koan 2

Bumbo asked his teacher, "Teacher, how can I find the path to correct comma use?"

The teacher closed his eyes and said, "Word."

2.   Commas when Joining Sentences

2.1.   *The tomatoes are ripe, but the carrots aren't.*
2.2.   *The caller was angry, so I want you to talk to her.*
2.3.   *The cost of gas is rising, and fewer people are driving on the highways.*

RULE D
Put a comma before a coordinating conjunction that joins two independent clauses.

Coordinating Conjunctions. The entire list of these conjunctions is *For, And, Nor, But, Or, Yet, So.* No other conjunctions fill this role.

Independent Clauses. For all practical purposes, this means a complete sentence. Usually when we talk about *independent clauses*, we are talking about an entire section of a sentence that could be a complete sentence.

The funny thing about this rule is that it's so easy to demonstrate and follow but so hard to describe.

Take a look at sample 2.1 above. It has 2 independent clauses: (1) *The tomatoes are ripe,* and (2) *the carrots aren't.* Sample 2.2 has these independent clauses: (1) *The caller was angry,* and (2) *I want you to talk to her.* Sample 2.3 has a similar structure.

If each of these independent clauses started with a capital letter and ended with a period, you would agree that they are complete sentences. In fact, we could re-write this rule as *Put a comma before the conjunction when joining two sentences.*

What the comma is doing here is letting the reader

know that the first complete thought is over and now the second one will begin. It provides a visual clue that you are about to provide a new, but related, idea.

In sample 2.3, the first complete thought (the first independent clause) is that the cost of gas is rising. The second complete thought (the second independent clause) is that fewer people are driving on the highway. The comma tells the reader where the first one ends and the second one begins.

2.4.   Dogs like running and jumping is good for them. *

Sample 2.4 shows how not following this rule can cause confusion. Many people, when first reading this sentence, would think that the main point is *Dogs like running and jumping*. This makes sense until you get to *is good for them*.

The reader may have to re-read the sentence to realize that it contains two complete thoughts: (1) *Dogs like running*, and (2), *jumping is good for them*. That's more work than the reader should have to do.

We want the reader to be thinking about the ideas we are communicating, not to be thinking about what the sentence means. Also, if you make your reader do a lot of work to understand, the reader will soon get tired of reading and either skim or ignore the rest.

When we use this comma consistently, we avoid potential confusion, such as caused by sample 2.4, and clearly identify the ideas we wish to communicate.

RULE E
Use commas as if implied words were present.

So far, using a comma before a coordinating conjunction that joins two independent clauses seems pretty easy. Applying this rule can be tricky when the sentence has implied words.

Implied words are left out of the sentence, usually because they are not needed to communicate the idea. This is a writing style issue, not a grammar issue.

When determining where to put commas, always consider what words, if any, are implied. Then put the commas in place as if those words were there. The most common implied word is *that*, as seen in the next example.

2.5.   *She knew that he would be late and she would miss dinner.*

Sample 2.5 looks like it has two independent clauses, but it is a trap. At first glance, the first independent clause seems to be *She knew that he would be late.* The second independent clause seems to be *she would miss dinner.* Based on Rule D, you might want to put a comma before *and*. However, this is not the case!

Let's look at what this sentence is communicating. She knew two things: (1) that he would be late, and (2) that she would miss dinner. This sentence has an implied *that*. If we were to put the implied words back into the sentence, the complete sentence would read *She knew that he would be late and that she would miss dinner.*

When we put the implied *that* back in the sentence, we see that this sentence doesn't have two independent clauses. The expression *that she would be late* is not an independent clause. It can't stand as a complete sentence. Because this sentence doesn't have two independent clauses, it doesn't need a comma.

2.6.   Tom bought flowers for his wife, and Fred, too.

Why is that comma after *wife* in sample 2.6? This sentence has the implied word *did*. The complete sentence, which contains two independent causes joined by *and*, is *Tom bought flowers for his wife, and Fred did, too.* When we put in the implied word, we see why that comma is needed. If we leave out the comma, the reader may think that Tom also bought flowers for Fred! (This will worry Tom's wife.)

RULE F
Don't use a comma before* because *when joining two independent clauses—unless needed by another rule.

Here's the other common trap I see with this rule. Based on a misunderstanding of Rule D, many people will put a comma before *because*, as in sample 2.7a.

2.7a. I was early, because I could not sleep. *
2.7b. I was early because I could not sleep.

Sample 2.7a is wrong for two reasons. First, *because* is not a coordinating conjunction, so the rule doesn't apply. Second, the word *because* is essential to the meaning of the words that follow it. It shows causality.

Unlike coordinating conjunctions that join two complete, separate thoughts, *because* is part of the meaning of the second part. *I could not sleep* isn't the whole idea. Without *because*, the overall meaning changes. Thus, sample 2.7b is the correct version.

In most cases, you won't need a comma before *because*. (Later chapters will show a few cases where you do.)

Koan 3

The teacher went to the platform to give his lesson on commas. He looked at the students, saying nothing. Then he wrote a comma on the wall and left.

"Ah," said Bumbo. "Missing words need commas, too!"

Koan 4

Bumbo asked his teacher, "Do all conjunctions need commas?"

The teacher immediately struck him.

"Why did you hit me?" Bumbo cried.

The teacher answered, "Because."

3.   Commas after Introductory Descriptions

3.1.   After visiting the vet, her dog was sleepy.
3.2.   If Mary likes cold soup, she will enjoy dinner.
3.3.   When the sun sets, the desert air cools.
3.4.   On Monday afternoon, the store will close early.

RULE G
Put a comma after introductory clauses and phrases.

Introductory clauses and phrases. These are phrases and clauses before the subject of the sentence (hence the name *introductory*) that tell something about the main action, such as when, where, how, and why it occurred.

Common words that start these introductory clauses and phrases include *after, although, as, because, before, even if, since, though, until, when, whether,* and *while.* Any complete sentence that starts with one of these, or similar, words has an introductory phrase or clause.

When the commas are in the correct places, these clauses and phrases are easy to find. In sample 3.1, the introductory phrase is *After visiting the vet.* It tells when the dog was sleepy. In sample 3.2, the introductory clause is *If Mary likes cold soup.* This one provides a condition for enjoying dinner.

Samples 3.3 and 3.4 also have an introductory phrase or clause that describes the main action.

Once we find the introductory phrase or clause, the rule is easy to apply: put a comma after it. That comma provides a clue to the reader that the descriptive part at the beginning is now over and that you are about to make your main point. In clear writing, the introductory phrase or clause is generally followed by the subject and main verb of the sentence.

Some writing style guides claim that you don't need the comma if the introductory phrase or clause is short, such as when it contains fewer than 5 words— unless it contributes to clarity. Why 5 words? This seems arbitrary. It is also subjective, which means you risk confusing the reader. The reader might not understand, even though you think the meaning is perfectly clear.

3.5.   *Although she gets unhappy going to the vet is necessary.* *

3.6.   *Although she gets unhappy, going to the vet is necessary.*

For example, when reading sample 3.5, you might think that the entire introductory clause is *Although she gets unhappy going to the vet*. This looks like an introductory clause, and you expect it to be followed by the subject of the sentence. Then you get to *is necessary*, which isn't the subject. Suddenly, the sentence no longer makes sense.

The problem is that the reader doesn't have any clues about when the description ends and the main point will begin. In fact, the introductory clause is *Although she gets unhappy*, which is only 4 words! If we follow the 5-word "rule" and leave out the comma, the reader may be confused.

The comma in sample 3.6 solves this problem. Now, the reader knows where the description ends and the main body of the sentence begins.

Even if some style guides claim that that comma is unnecessary in some situations, it will never be wrong. To be consistent, and to increase the likelihood that your reader will understand you, always use it.

RULE H
Don't separate the descriptive clause or phrase if it occurs at the end of the sentence.

3.7.   *While swimming, she swallowed a frog.*
3.8.   *She swallowed a frog while swimming.*

On the other hand, if you move that phrase or clause to the end of the sentence, you will no longer need a comma. When we move the introductory phrase in sample 3.7 to the end of the sentence in sample 3.8, we don't need the comma.

Later, we'll discuss a specific case where we will separate an ending phrase with a comma, but, as you will see, it is quite different from this case.

Koan 5

Bumbo was speaking to a fellow student and said, "Surely, short clauses are not important enough for commas."

The teacher walked over to Bumbo, looked up at him, and said, "Who are you to judge?"

4.   Commas with Interjections

4.1.   Yes, we can fill this order on time.
4.2.   Oh, I must have misunderstood your request.
4.3.   I have, alas, more than I need.

RULE I
Separate interjections with commas.

Interjections. *Interjections* are words that express a reaction to information, most typically an emotional reaction. An introductory interjection occurs at the beginning of a sentence.

Sample interjections are *ahem, alas, bravo, dang, darn, hey, no, oh, oops, shh, well, whew,* and *yes.*

This rule is quite simple to understand and apply. An interjection has no grammatical function in a sentence, so it must be separated from the rest of the sentence with commas. To check this, remove it from the sentence; the sentence will still be grammatically correct.

Typically, interjections are used at the beginning of a sentence, as in samples 4.1 and 4.2. If the reaction being expressed is very strong, you can follow an introductory interjection with an exclamation mark. However, I don't recommend you do this in formal writing.

In fact, most interjections are not appropriate for formal writing, except some cases, such as *yes* and *no.* Most interjections express the writer's emotional response, not objective information. Interjections are more common when writing dialogue or quoting someone.

Sample 4.3 contains an internal interjection. I also don't recommend using internal interjections. Not only do they inject an emotional reaction but also they interrupt the flow of information you wish to communicate.

4.4. Well, you did say that you are going.
4.5. He completed the task well before the deadline.

As one caution, some words can serve as either interjections or other parts of speech, depending on how they are used. In sample 4.4, *well* is an interjection and is followed by a comma. This fits the rule for this chapter. In sample 4.5, however, *well* is an adverb describing *before*.

When considering whether or not to use a comma, and where the comma should go, think about what the words are communicating.

Koan 6

"Have you learned much about commas?" the teacher asked his students.

"No teacher," Bumbo wrote in reply.

The teacher became sad and said, "Ah, if you use a comma, you will have a teacher."

5.   Commas with Appositives

5.1. The package, a brown box with no return address, sat in the storeroom for weeks.
5.2. My car, a 2011 Honda Accord, needs cleaning.
5.3. Bob's daughter Sara graduated last year. (Bob has more than one daughter.)

FIRST, APPOSITIVES

The term *appositive* is new to most people, so let's take a little time to figure out what it means. (In all my writing classes, I ask students if they know this term. Only once did someone know it.) Once we understand the term *appositive*, we will use it to discuss commas.

Appositive. An *appositive* is a word, phrase, or clause that renames something just written; the appositive is the same thing as whatever it renames. An appositive is considered to be *in apposition* to the thing it is renaming.

Even if the term *appositive* is new to you, you can probably spot appositives easily.

In sample 5.1, the phrase *a brown box with no return address* renames, or is another way of saying, *package*. Here, *package* and *a brown box with no return address* are the same thing. Because of this, we know that *a brown box with no return address* is an appositive. It is in apposition to *package*.

This is similar to sample 5.2. Here, *a 2011 Honda Accord* renames, or has the same meaning as, *my car*. Thus, *a 2011 Honda Accord* is an appositive.

The appositives in samples 5.1 and 5.2 are *non-restrictive appositives* because the appositives and the words they rename are a perfect one-to-one match. Everything described by the appositive equals everything described by the term that the appositive renames.

With a non-restrictive appositive, you are not restricting, or limiting, the readers' attention to one thing among several. You are not indicating one thing from a group of things. Rather, you are providing additional details.

In sample 5.2, *a 2011 Honda Accord* exactly describes *my car.* I have no cars other than the 2011 Honda Accord. Everything described by *my car* is also described by *a 2011 Honda Accord*, a perfect one-to-one match. Sample 5.1 works the same way.

Sample 5.3 does not have a non-restrictive appositive. It has a *restrictive appositive.* Bob has more than one daughter, so *Sara* is not a perfect one-to-one match with *daughter.* In this sample, we are restricting, or limiting, the readers' attention from the group of daughters to one particular daughter named *Sara.*

Here's another way to differentiate restrictive and non-restrictive appositives.

Restrictive: Specifies which thing.
Non-restrictive: Provides additional description or renames.

RULE J
Separate non-restrictive appositives with commas.

Now that we have learned to find appositives, following this rule is easy. If you have a non-restrictive appositive, separate it from the rest of the sentence with commas.

In samples 5.1 and 5.2, the appositives are embedded in the sentence. They are separated from the rest of the sentence by commas, both before and after.

The first comma gives the reader a clue that we're about to provide some extra information. The second comma lets the reader know that we're getting back to the main point.

5.4.   I sent the letter to my best friend, John.

Sample 5.4 is a little different. In this sample, the non-restrictive appositive is *John*. *John* is in apposition to *my best friend*. It is the last word of the sentence, so we only need the comma before *John*.

RULE K
Don't use commas to separate restrictive appositives.

Non-restrictive appositives need commas. Restrictive appositives don't. Non-restrictive appositives can be removed from the sentence without losing essential content. Restrictive appositives can't.

Sample 5.3 provides a good example of this. Bob has other daughters, so *Sara* tells us which daughter. As such, *Sara* is not separated by commas. If we use commas around *Sara*, we make *Sara* non-restrictive, a perfect one-to-one match with *daughter*, and his other daughters cease to exist!

Koan 7

Bumbo wrote a letter to his parents. At the end of the letter he wrote, "Please give my regards to my sister, Vera."

His teacher asked, "How many sisters do you have?"

Bumbo answered, "Two."

"Oh, you wicked student!" his teacher cried. "Your comma just killed one."

---

6.   Commas with Side Comments

6.1.   *The new features, I am sure, will confuse buyers.*
6.2.   *The legislative budget proposal, in spite of our protests, will become law.*

RULE L
Separate interpolated asides with commas.

Interpolated aside. An *interpolated aside* is a word, phrase, or clause that gives the writer's opinion about the idea being communicated in the sentence. It is a side comment injected in the sentence and is not part of the main idea being expressed.

Sample 6.1 contains the interpolated aside *I am sure.* This statement gives the writer's opinion of the buyers' reactions. Sample 6.2 contains the interpolated aside *in spite of our protests.* This statement gives the writer's feelings about the budget proposal. In both cases, the interpolated asides are not the main points or ideas being expressed in the sentence. Rather, they express the writer's thoughts, feelings, and opinions about the main point or idea.

Once you know what you're looking for, following this rule is simple. Find the interpolated asides and put commas around them, before and after, to separate them from the main sentence.

From an editing perspective, I generally recommend leaving out interpolated asides. They interrupt the communication, and they change the readers' attention from your ideas to your opinions about those ideas, from the point you are trying to make to you.

A better approach is either to move the aside to the beginning of the sentence or to provide your opinion in the next sentence.

6.3.   I am sure the new features will confuse the buyers.

*6.4.   In spite of our protests, the legislative budget proposal will
become law.*

Sample 6.3 uses the interpolated aside as the main
subject and verb. Sample 6.4 uses the interpolated
aside as an introductory phrase, followed by a comma.

7.   Commas with Names

7.1.   John, please bring me your files.
7.2.   I am sure, Mr. President, that the general public won't mind.

RULE M
When directly addressing someone, place commas around his or her name.

When you use someone's name (or title in place of a name), you interrupt the message of the sentence with that name. Because you are making an interruption without adding content, separate the name from the rest of the sentence with commas.

The writer in sample 7.1 is directly addressing *John*. The writer in sample 7.2 is directly addressing *Mr. President*. Thus, both names are separated with commas. In fact, using commas with names is nearly the same as using commas with interpolated asides (Chapter 6), and for nearly the same reason.

7.3.   This is my dog, Chuck.

I have one caution about this comma use. The name may appear to be an appositive, as in sample 7.3. In this sample, who is *Chuck*? Is Chuck the name of the dog or the person being addressed? The reader will likely know the difference, but you may need to revise your sentence to prevent this confusion.

Koan 8

Bumbo was interrupted by another student.

"I met your brother, Bumbo," said the student.

*"How can that be?" Bumbo asked. "**My** name is Bumbo."*

---

8.   Commas with *Therefore, Too,* and Other Conjunctive Adverbs

8.1.   *She left early. Therefore, he was lonely.*
8.2.   *The town flooded; as such, the field is unusable.*
8.3.   *I, too, am ready for dinner.*

RULE N
Separate conjunctive adverbs with commas.

Conjunctive Adverb. A conjunctive adverb shows how the idea in one sentence or independent clause is related, or connected, to the idea in the previous sentence or independent clause. Conjunctive adverbs include such words as *additionally, finally, however, indeed, in fact, rather, similarly, therefore, thus,* and *too.*

Without the conjunctive adverb in sample 8.1, the two sentences will present two unrelated ideas. The conjunctive adverb connects the idea in sentence two to the idea in sentence one. *Therefore* indicates a cause and effect relationship between the two sentences. It indicates how *he was lonely* relates to *She left early.*

When the conjunctive adverb is at the beginning of the sentence, as with *Therefore* in sample 8.1, it needs to be followed by a comma to separate it from the rest of the sentence.

In sample 8.2, the conjunctive adverb *as such* is the beginning of the second independent clause. (Notice the semicolon that joins the two clauses.) It is also followed by a comma to separate it from the information that follows it.

Samples 8.1 and 8.2 demonstrate the most common placement for the conjunctive adverbs: at the beginning of the sentence. However, like all adverbs, conjunctive adverbs can be moved to various locations in an independent clause.

Sample 8.3, with *too* inside the sentence, demonstrates how the conjunctive adverb can be placed within the sentence. This sample also follows the rule. The conjunctive adverb *too* is separated from the rest of the sentence with commas before and after it.

8.4.   I am ready for dinner, too.

The comma with the word *too* causes a lot of confusion when *too* is used at the end of a sentence. If you put *too* at the end of the sentence, it will still need to be separated from the rest of the sentence with a comma, as seen in sample 8.4.

Some style guides state that the comma is optional when *too* is the last word. Others say it is required because it follows the rule about separating conjunctive adverbs with commas. However, *optional* isn't the same thing as *wrong*, which means your safest strategy is always to use it. The sentence won't be considered wrong if you use the comma, but you may be criticized if you leave it out. This is why I recommend always using optional commas.

8.5.   Therefore, he, too, will go.
8.6.   Therefore, he will go.

This use of commas, perhaps more than any other use, can create sentences that sound choppy. Each comma creates a slight pause, so when you put commas around internal conjunctive adverbs, you may end up with a sentence that has many pauses.

Sample 8.5 contains only five words, but it also contains three commas. It has a comma after nearly every word. That's a lot of commas! It looks overly complicated, and it will sound choppy if you read it aloud.

My advice in situations like this is to revise the sentence. You can find a different way to express your idea, re-order the words, or leave out the conjunctive adverb if it is not necessary. Sample 8.6 used the third approach because *too* is implied by the sentence.

RULE O
Don't use conjunctive adverbs to join independent clauses.

A common mistake when the second independent clause starts with a conjunctive adverb is to join the two independent clauses with only a comma.

8.7.   The town flooded, as such, the field is unusable. *

This creates a comma splice, which is always an error. Sample 8.7 makes this mistake. Instead, use a comma followed by a coordinating conjunction (see chapter 2), a semicolon (see sample 8.2), or a colon. You can also make two separate sentences (see sample 8.1).

Koan 9
Bumbo approached his teacher with a concerned look on his face.

"Teacher," he said, "some commas seem optional. How do I know whether or not to use them?"

In response, the teacher asked him, "Two bridges cross the river. One bridge is missing steps, and the other is whole. Which do you use?"

9.   Commas with Adjective Pairs

9.1.   We had a hot, dry summer.
9.2.   A large brown bear is loose in the park.

RULE P
Place a comma between coordinate adjectives.

You have two adjectives together. Do you or don't you put a comma between them? If they are coordinate adjectives, you do.

Coordinate Adjectives. Adjectives are coordinate if they meet two criteria: (1) You can place *and* between the two words, and the sentence means the same thing, and (2) You can reverse their order, and the sentence means the same thing.

Sample 9.1 has the adjectives *hot* and *dry*, both used to describe *summer*. If we write *We had a hot and dry summer*, the sentence makes sense. It also makes sense if we write *We had a dry, hot summer*. The adjectives meet both criteria, so we know they are coordinate and put a comma between them.

To native English speakers, the two revised sentences will sound like natural speech, and the two criteria are likely sufficient to identify coordinate adjectives. For a more technical explanation, we can examine the *Royal Order of Adjectives*.

(If these criteria and revisions make sense to you, skip the next section and go to Rule Q.)

Royal Order of Adjectives. This is the order in which native English speakers naturally use adjectives in speech and writing. Although exceptions exist, such as to emphasize specific characteristics, this order is generally true.

The Royal Order of Adjectives is as follows.

1. Determiners: Words that indicate which one (e.g., *this, the, a, my, her*)

2. Observations: Subjective descriptions (e.g., *fast, decrepit, easy, beautiful, inexpensive*)

3. Size: Physical descriptions of size (e.g., *large, small, huge, miniscule*)

4. Shape: Physical descriptions of shape (e.g., *round, square, lean, misshapen, long, oblong*)

5. Age: Adjectives that indicate age (e.g., *old, new, three-year-old, antique*)

6. Color: Physical descriptions of color (e.g., *red, blue, creamy, hazy, fuchsia*)

7. Nationality: Originating location (e.g., *American, French, European*)

8. Material: What something is made of (e.g., *silk, cardboard, rubber, sand, wooden, cream*)

9. Type: The specific type of the thing (e.g., *rocking* [horse], *digital* [phone], *acoustic* [guitar]); may be considered part of the name of the thing described

The Royal Order of Adjectives indicates that *The* [determiner] *black* [color] *sand* [material] *painting* will sound natural but that *The sand black painting* will not. Similarly, *Her* [determiner] *large* [size] *wooden* [material] *antique* [type] *clock* will sound more natural than *Her wooden antique large clock.*

The Royal Order of Adjectives is important to understanding coordinate adjectives. If you write two or more adjectives of the same type, they will be coordinate, and you will need a comma between them.

9.3.   I have a fast, inexpensive car.

For example, *fast* and *inexpensive* are both observation adjectives. This means they are coordinate when used together, as in sample 9.3, and need a comma. We can also apply the two criteria to check this. We can put *and* between them: *I have a fast and inexpensive car.* We can reverse their order: *I have an inexpensive, fast car.*

RULE Q
Leave out the comma between coordinate adjectives to make them non-coordinate and change the meaning.

The comma between coordinate adjectives indicates that they both equally describe something. In sample 9.3, *fast* and *inexpensive* equally describe *car*. If you leave out the comma, however, you change the meaning of the sentence.

9.4.   I have a fast inexpensive car.

In sample 9.4, you still indicate that *inexpensive* describes *car*, but you also indicate that *fast* describes *inexpensive car.* You tell the reader that your inexpensive car is fast. A *fast inexpensive car* is different than a *slow inexpensive car*, for example. The comma, or its absence, makes a lot of difference in your meaning.

If you're using the Royal Order of Adjectives, you will

see that when you leave out the comma, *inexpensive* becomes a type adjective, rather than an observation adjective. *Inexpensive* is a type of car in sample 9.4, making *fast* and *inexpensive* different types of adjectives, and you don't need the comma.

I know this is getting confusing, so I'll summarize the main points.

1) If the two adjectives equally describe something, they will meet the two criteria. Put a comma between them.

2) If the first adjective describes the next adjective and thing together, they won't meet the two criteria. Don't put a comma between them. This leads us to the following rule.

RULE R
Don't place a comma between non-coordinate adjectives.

Use the same two criteria to determine whether or not two adjectives are coordinate. If the adjectives don't meet the criteria, don't use a comma. This rule is, simply, the opposite of Rule P.

Look at sample 9.2. No comma is between *large* and *brown*. If we change their order, as in *A brown large bear*, it doesn't make sense or, at the least, changes the meaning of the sentence. From this we know that these two adjectives are not coordinate, and we don't put a comma between them. If we use the Royal Order of Adjectives, we also realize that these are different types of adjectives.

9.5. The original American flag is on display.

The two adjectives in sample 9.4 are not coordinate. We cannot write *the American original flag* or *The original and American flag* without changing the meaning of the sentence. Thus, we don't add a comma.

If we use the Royal Order of Adjectives, we see that these are different types of adjectives. *Original* is an observation adjective, and *American* is a nationality adjective. They don't need a comma.

RULE S
Don't put a comma between an adjective and the thing it describes.

Commas separate things. However, the adjectives should not be separated from the things they describe. For this reason, you don't use a comma between the final adjective and the noun it describes, regardless of how many adjectives you use.

9.6.   These old, red, wooden, frames are still my favorites.*

Surprisingly, this mistake is common, though it is so simple to avoid. If no words are between the adjectives and the word being described, you will never need a comma in that position.

In sample 9.6, for example, the adjectives are describing *frames*. No words are between the final adjective *wooden* and *frames*, so no comma should be there.

Koan 10

Bumbo and a friend were walking wearing matching robes. They were arguing about who should walk in front.

Bumbo asked a passing teacher, "What order should we walk in, teacher?"

The teacher answered, "You all look the same to me."

10. Commas with *Which* and *Who*

10.1. I purchased a Geiger counter, which is a device for measuring radioactivity.

10.2. The iPhone, which was developed by Apple Computers, is a remarkable piece of technology.

10.3. John Wilson, who founded the company, was a generous man.

10.4. Beethoven, who was deaf when older, continued composing until his death in 1827.

We'll look at commas with *which* first, and then we'll study commas with *who*. These two uses are together because they are based on the same principle: separate non-restrictive phrases and clauses with commas.

RULE T
Use commas to separate non-restrictive phrases and clauses starting with which.

This rule has some redundancy. If you use *which* correctly, every descriptive phrase or clause that starts with *which* will be non-restrictive. Also, every non-restrictive phrase or clause is separated from the rest of the sentence by commas. Thus, every phrase or clause that begins with *which* will be separated from the rest of the sentence with commas.

Chapter 5 has an explanation of restrictive and non-restrictive phrases. For example, sample 5.2 reads *My car, a 2011 Honda Accord, needs cleaning* and contains the non-restrictive phrase *a 2011 Honda Accord*. Here's the summary from Chapter 5 about non-restrictive and restrictive phrases and clauses:

Restrictive: Specifies which thing
Non-restrictive: Provides additional description or renames

Let's see how this works with the word *which*.

The main sentence in sample 10.1 is *I purchased a Geiger counter*. The phrase *which is a device for measuring radioactivity* provides an additional description of *Geiger counter* that is not necessary for understanding the central meaning of the sentence.

It doesn't tell us which Geiger counter we are writing about. Rather, it renames *Geiger counter*. Because of this, *which is a device for measuring radioactivity* is a non-restrictive phrase and needs to be separated from the rest of the sentence by a comma.

(If we needed to indicate which Geiger counter we're writing about, we would have used *that* and not *which*, resulting in a restrictive phrase.)

Sample 10.2 works similarly. The main sentence is *The iPhone is a remarkable piece of technology*. The phrase *which was developed by Apple Computers* provides additional description of *iPhone* and is not essential for understanding the central meaning of the sentence. It doesn't tell us which iPhone we're writing about, so it is a non-restrictive phrase and needs to be separated from the rest of the sentence with commas.

In brief, if you use *which* correctly to start non-restrictive phrases and clauses, you will always need a comma before *which*.

10.5. *The iPhone, developed by Apple Computers, is a remarkable piece of technology.*

We already know from Rule E to use commas as if implied words were present. That rule means we need the commas in sample 10.5 around the restrictive phrase *developed by Apple Computers*. This phrase has the implied words *which was*.

Here's the trap, however. Let's say you're typing along happily, and you use the word *which* without the comma. Your word processor puts an insulting green line under it to indicate an error. The recommended solution is to put a comma before *which*. Before you do that, make sure *which* is the correct word. The problem might not be the missing comma but the wrong word. Maybe you need *that* instead.

RULE U
Use commas to separate non-restrictive phrases and clauses starting with **who.**

Unlike the word *which*, the word *who* may start either a non-restrictive or restrictive phrase or clause. You have to think carefully about what you are trying to say.

Samples 10.3 and 10.4 use *who* to start non-restrictive clauses. They work exactly the same as samples 10.1 and 10.2.

In sample 10.3, *who founded the company* provides additional information about *John Wilson*. In sample 10.4, *who was deaf when older* provides additional description of *Beethoven*. These clauses don't tell us which *John Wilson* or which *Beethoven* we mean, so they are non-restrictive and need to be separated from the rest of the sentence with commas.

In these samples, *who* is doing the same thing as *which*.

RULE V
Don't use commas to separate restrictive phrases and clauses starting with **who.**

Sometimes, the clause starting with *who* **does** tell us which person you are writing about. In this case, the clause will be restrictive, which means you don't need the commas.

10.6. *Talk to the man who sits at the first desk.*

Some writers will mistakenly apply Rule U to put a comma in front of every *who*. This is only required if the *who* clause does not tell which person you are writing about.

In sample 10.6, *who sits at the first desk* tells which man. That clause is essential to understanding what the sentence means. Without that information, the reader will not know to whom he or she should talk.

Remember:

Non-restrictive: Renames or provides a non-essential description. *Which* always starts a non-restrictive phrase or clause. *Who* might start a non-restrictive clause. Commas required.

Restrictive: Provides essential information to know which person or thing you are writing about. *That* starts a restrictive phrase or clause. *Who* might start a restrictive clause. No commas required.

Koan 11

Bumbo stood silently before his teacher, who was writing a lesson about commas. Finally, the teacher looked up from his desk.

"It's me, Bumbo," Bumbo said.

"I already know which one you are," the teacher answered. "Go stand outside."

11.   Commas with Final Descriptions

11.1. The club is disbanding, based on this letter.
11.2. He saw the corpse, swimming in the lake.
11.3. He drove all day, unable to wait longer.
11.4. The legislation is dead, not delayed.
11.5. The audience seemed tired, an understandable response to the boring 3-hour lecture.

RULE W
Use commas to separate final descriptions that don't refer to the immediately preceding text.

To vary sentence structure, you may put a descriptive phrase at the end of a sentence. However, readers will usually link descriptions to the closest preceding text. This is not always accurate, so we use a comma to prevent the reader from doing this.

The comma separates the description from the preceding text to show that they are not connected. Sample 11.1–11.5 each show a different way a comma separates the final description.

In sample 11.1, the letter states that the club is disbanding. If we leave out the comma, the sentence will state that the club is disbanding because of the letter, as seen in sample 11.6.

11.6. The club is disbanding based on this letter.

This indicates that the letter, or its contents, is causing the club to disband because *disbanding* is described by *based on this letter*. However, with the comma in sample 11.1 we know that *disbanding* is not described by *based on this letter*, leading to the desired interpretation.

Sample 11.2 works in a similar way. If we leave out

the comma, the reader will think *swimming in the lake* is a description of *the corpse*, as if the corpse were swimming in the lake. Rather, *swimming in the lake* is a description of *He*. To prevent the incorrect, and odd, interpretation, we must separate the final description.

RULE X
Use commas to separate non-grammatical final descriptions.

In other cases, the final description is not grammatically connected to the preceding sentence. Similar to Rule W, this can happen when the final description refers to the subject or main verb but not to the words that immediately precede the description.

In sample 11.3, *unable to wait longer* describes the subject *He*, not *drove all day*. Unlike samples 11.1 and 11.2, however, we cannot remove the comma and still have a grammatically correct sentence, as follows in sample 11.7.

11.7. He drove all day unable to wait longer. *

These are a form of *free modifiers*, a descriptive phrase that can be moved around in the sentence. If they can't be moved around without making the sentence confusing, they are not free modifiers and don't need a comma. If they can be moved around, they are free modifiers, and they need commas.

RULE Y
Use commas to separate final coordinate expressions.

From Rule P, we know to put a comma between coordinate adjectives, such as in sample 9.1. This can also affect how we use commas with final descriptions.

If the final two descriptive phrases or expressions equally describe the same thing, they are coordinate, and we separate them with a comma.

11.8. The legislation is dead. The legislation is not delayed.

In sample 11.8, we see that *dead* and *not delayed* both describe *legislation.* We could write this in two sentences, as I have here, or we can combine them and end the sentence with both descriptions, as I did in sample 11.4. When I combine the sentences, these two descriptions are coordinate and require a comma.

RULE Z
Use a comma to indicate a shift in focus at the end of the sentence.

This is fairly simple. Take a look at sample 11.5. The main sentence is about the audience. However, the final description is not so much about the audience as it is about the boring lecture. This is a shift in the focus of the sentence. As such, it is separated by a comma.

Koan 12

A group of tourists were visiting the school, and Bumbo was curious about them.

"Teacher," he asked, "may I follow those tourists?"

The teacher replied, "Not without a comma."

12. Commas with Parenthetical Expressions and Absolute Phrases

12.1. *The new mall, I have heard, will be huge.*
12.2. *This economic forecast model, compared to other models, shows flat growth.*
12.3. *The meeting finished, the board members left.*

RULE AA
Separate parenthetical expressions with commas.

Parenthetical expression. These are expressions that do not add essential content for understanding the sentence, such as an off-topic comment or a phrase inserted in a sentence that breaks the flow of the idea. These expressions may be placed in parentheses; hence the name.

This rule is something of a catch-all, a grammatical version of "other duties as assigned." Many phrases and clauses are considered parenthetical expressions, including appositives, direct addresses, interpolated asides, and interjections.

Basically, any expression, description, comment, etc. that interrupts the flow of ideas, that can be moved around in the sentence, and that can be placed in parentheses without confusing the reader needs to be separated from the rest of the sentence with commas.

In sample 12.1, the parenthetical expression is *I have heard*. This is not part of the idea being expressed in the sentence. It can be moved to the front or end of the sentence. And it could be placed in parentheses. As such, it is separated from the rest of the sentence with commas, one before and one after. Also, if I had written it at the end of the sentence, I would still need to separate it from the rest of the sentence.

In sample 12.2, the parenthetical expression is *compared to other models*. Wherever I put it in the sentence, it will need to be separated by commas.

12.4. Compared to other models, this economic forecast model shows flat growth.

12.5. This economic forecast model shows flat growth, compared to other models.

Sample 12.4 uses the parenthetical expression as an introductory adverbial phrase (Rule G), and sample 12.5 uses it as a non-grammatical final description (Rule X). Because it is a parenthetical expression, no matter where it is in the sentence, it needs to be separated from the rest of the sentence with commas.

RULE AB
Separate absolute phrases with commas.

Absolute phrase. An absolute phrase modifies, or describes, the entire sentence, not any particular word in the sentence. It contains a noun and a participle, and it may contain additional descriptive terms.

Participle. A participle is a form of a verb being used as an adjective. For example, *burning* is used as an adjective in *the burning building*. It describes *building* and cannot be used as a verb unless you add another verb, as in *The building is burning*.

Absolute phrases are a form of parenthetical expression, which is why they are included in this chapter. Because they describe the entire contents of a sentence, they, too, can be moved to various locations in the sentence, and they, too, are separated from the rest of the sentence with commas.

Sample 12.3 contains the absolute phrase *The meeting finished*. This absolute phrase contains the noun *meeting* and the participle *finished*, which is being used as an adjective to describe *meeting*. The absolute phrase relates to everything in the sentence, not any particular word. It describes the entire situation in which *the board members left*.

The absolute phrase can also be moved to other places in the sentence, and the sentence will still make sense, as in sample 12.6.

12.6. The board members left, the meeting finished.

Once we realize that *the meeting finished* is not an independent clause with a subject and a verb but an absolute phrase with a noun and a predicate, we will understand that this is correct and not a comma splice. We're not joining two independent clauses with only a comma.

Regardless of where the absolute phrase is, it needs to be separated from the rest of the sentence with commas.

Koan 13

Bumbo asked, "How can I understand absolute phrases?"

His teacher asked in response, "What is the universe?"

"It's what is all around us," Bumbo replied, still confused.

The teacher nodded sagely and said, "Meditate on the universe, and you will be enlightened."

13. Commas with Dates, Addresses, Ages, and Titles

13.1. I met her on February 14, 1949, in the park.

13.2. People in Fairbanks, Alaska, are accustomed to cold weather.

13.3. John Brown, aged 14, knew all about girls.

13.4. David Bowman, MA, MBA, wrote this book.

RULE AC
Put commas around the year when the month and day are included.

When you write a date and include the month, day, and year, the year needs to be separated with commas, both before and after. Sample 13.1 gives an example of this. The common mistake is to leave out the comma after the year.

RULE AD
Use commas to separate all major elements of an address.

If you write the street and city (town, etc.), put a comma between them. If you write the city and state, put a comma between them. If you write the state and country, put a comma between them. And so forth. Unless you only write the street number and name, you also need to put a comma after the final element in the address.

Sample 13.2 includes the city and state. The state name *Alaska* is separated from the city name *Fairbanks* with a comma. Notice, also, the comma after *Alaska*.

RULE AE
Put commas around ages if they are not part of the grammatical structure.

When you put the age after a name, and when the age is not part of the main sentence, as in sample 13.3, it becomes a parenthetical expression. We know from Rule AA that parenthetical expressions are separated from the rest of the sentence with commas, so we know to separate the age with commas.

13.5. John Brown was 14 years old. He knew everything there is to know about girls.

Sample 13.5 also has the age after the name. However, in this sample, the age is part of the main sentence, is part of the grammatical structure, and cannot be removed. Here, the age is essential information, not parenthetical. As such, no commas are needed.

Another way to write the age after the name is as follows.

13.6. John Brown, 14, knew all about girls.

This is more common in journalistic writing than in other styles. This age, too, is separated from the rest of the sentence with commas.

RULE AF
Put commas around titles if they are not part of the grammatical structure.

Sample 13.4, which has the titles *MA, MBA.*, shows the correct use of commas with titles. Titles that follow names work exactly like ages, and generally like sample 13.6. The common mistake is to leave out the comma after the title.

14. Commas with Quotations

14.1. "The budget has been depleted," the CEO said.
14.2. The CEO said, "The budget has been depleted," and then he submitted his resignation.
14.3. When you say "chowder," "chocolate," or "cheese," my mouth waters.

RULE AG
Separate quoted material from the main sentence with commas.

Quotations are not part of the main sentence, so they need to be separated from the main sentence with commas. In sample 14.1, the main sentence is *the CEO said*. A comma separates the CEO's statement from the main sentence.

Sample 14.2 has two commas, one before the quotation and one after. The second comma is required by Rule D: Put a comma before a coordinating conjunction that joins two independent clauses. The first comma, however, separates the CEO's statement from the main sentence.

RULE AH
Put the comma inside the final quotation mark.

Inside or outside? This is a common question when using quotation marks. The answer is simple: Inside. Assuming you are using U.S. writing conventions, this will always be the case, even when the comma is not part of the quoted material.

(If you're using British writing conventions, the comma goes outside the quotation marks unless it is part of the quoted material.)

Take another look at sample 14.1. We now know that

the quoted statement needs a comma to separate it from the main sentence. That comma goes **inside** the final quotation mark. We see this again in sample 14.2.

Sample 14.3 is a bit different. Here, we have a series of three words. Rule A tells us to separate every item in a series with a comma, and sample 14.3 follows this rule.

We put quotation marks around those words to indicate that we are referring to them as words, not using them as part of the sentence. These commas, too, go inside the quotation marks. This may seem counter-intuitive. After all, these are not quotations. The quotation marks indicate that these are discrete words, so you might think the quotation marks only go around the words.

Even in cases like this, the comma goes inside the final quotation marks.

When discussing words, as in sample 14.3, you can avoid this problem altogether by using italics. Instead of putting quotation marks around the words, put them in italics, as follows.

14.4. *When you say* **chowder, chocolate,** *or* **cheese,** *my mouth waters.*

Koan 14:

Bumbo knocked on the door of the Temple of Meaning and said, "May I come in?"

"Do you bring a comma?" his teacher replied.

"Yes," Bumbo answered.

"Ah," said the teacher, "bring it inside."

15. No Commas with *Either...Or* and Other Correlative Pairs

15.1. I knew either he would find the boxes where he had left them or he would find them some other place.

15.2. Not only will the president attend but also the vice president will attend.

RULE AI
Don't separate the two halves of a correlative pair with a comma.

Correlative pair. A correlative pair (or a pair of correlative conjunctions, to be exact) is a pair of words that join equal parts of sentences. Samples include *not only...but also, neither...nor, whether...or*, and *both... and*.

The two parts of a correlative pair are required for the sentence to be complete and grammatically correct. Because they are both required, the second part cannot be separated by a comma.

Sample 15.1 contains the correlative pair *either...or.* The first part, *either he would find the boxes where he had left them*, requires the second part, *or he would find them some other place*, to be complete. You could not, for example, put a period after the first part. The common mistake is to put a comma before *or*, thus separating the two parts.

Sample 15.2 contains the correlative pair *not only... but also*. Of all the comma mistakes with correlative pairs, this one is the most common. Don't use a comma before *but also* unless required by another rule.

15.3. Not only will the president attend, as stated in his letter, but also the vice president will attend.

If we follow rule AI, we might question the comma before *but* also in sample 15.3. However, that comma is not separating the two halves of the correlative pair. Rather, it is separating the parenthetical expression *as stated in his letter* from the rest of the sentence.

The two commas in sample 15.3 are required by rule AA: Separate parenthetical expressions with commas. They are not there because of the correlative pair. If we remove *as stated in his letter*, those two commas also disappear.

15.4. *Neither Tommy, my younger brother, nor his wife live in the U.S.*

Sample 15.4 has the correlative pair *neither...nor*. This sentence has a comma before the second part of the correlative pair. That comma and the one before it are there because of the appositive *my younger brother*. These two commas, one before and one after *my younger brother*, follow Rule J: Separate non-restrictive appositives with commas.

If we remove the appositive, and the two commas it requires, we won't have a comma before the second part of the correlative pair. The commas are required by the appositive, not by the correlative pair.

Koan 15

Bumbo wrote a letter to his teacher, stating, "Thank you for teaching me about commas. I now use them as often as possible."

When the teacher received the letter, he tore it down the middle and sent the first half back to Bumbo.

"Ah," said Bumbo, "not all commas are needed."

16. No Commas between Subjects and Predicates

16.1. The clerk who noticed the open vault when the bank opened at 7:00 Monday morning was later charged with theft.

16.2. After years of failed trials, the company that had the greatest success patented the electric car.

Predicate. The *predicate* is, for all practical purposes, the main verb and everything that follows it. The predicate in sample 16.1 begins with *was*. The predicate in sample 16.2 begins with *patented*.

RULE AJ
Don't use a comma to separate the predicate from the subject.

A sentence must contain two things to be complete: a subject and a predicate. The subject tells who or what the sentence is about, and the predicate tells what the subject is or does. If either part is missing, the sentence will be a fragment.

Commas separate parts of sentences. However, a sentence must have a subject and a predicate. The predicate, as a required element, should not be separated from the subject. Writers often make this mistake when the subject is long or complex.

The subject in sample 16.1 is long and it has its own verbs: *The clerk who noticed the open vault when the bank opened at 7:00 Monday morning*. This complex subject has the subject–verb combinations *who noticed* and *bank opened*. Because the subject is complex, some writers will put a comma after it. The predicate in 16.1 is *was later charged with theft*. As you can see, no comma is between the subject and predicate.

Perhaps writers do this because after reading a long, complex subject, they find that they need to take a breath. The "put a comma where you pause" rule is risky and, as in this case, may lead to an error.

Sample 16.2 is similar. Once we ignore the introductory phase *After years of failed trials*, we see that the subject is *the company that had the greatest success* and that the predicate is *patented the electric car*. As with sample 16.1, no comma is between the subject and predicate.

16.3. My uncle, who had a large boat, took the family for a picnic.

Based on Rule AJ, we might question the comma before the predicate *took the family for a picnic* in sample 16.3. That comma and the previous comma are there because of the non-restrictive phrase *who had a large boat*. We learned with Rule U to use commas to separate non-restrictive clauses beginning with *who*.

As such, those two commas are there to separate the non-restrictive phrase, not to separate the predicate from the subject. If we remove the non-restrictive phrase, those commas also disappear.

Koan 16

Bumbo sat motionless in the Temple of Meaning. His teacher asked what he was doing.

"I am learning to use commas," Bumbo told him.

"You foolish student," the teacher exclaimed. "If you do not act on what you know, your life will never be complete."

17. No Commas between Compound Predicates

17.1. The phones were ringing all day and were silent all night.
17.2. The files you sent were infected with some sort of virus and could not be opened on our system.

Compound predicate. Some subjects have two predicates, each of which describes a particular action. We call them a *compound predicate*. Writers use this strategy to combine similar sentences.

RULE AK
Don't use a comma to separate two parts of a compound predicate.

This is simpler than it sounds. Sample 17.1 has one subject, *The phones*, and two main actions, *were ringing all day* and *were silent all night*.

As we saw with Rule AJ, we cannot separate a predicate from the subject with a comma. If we put a comma between the two predicates, we separate the second predicate from the subject.

Sample 17.2 also has two predicates: *were infected with some sort of virus* and *could not be opened on our system*. No comma separates them, so no comma separates the second predicate from the subject.

As with Rule AJ, however, sometimes we will have a comma before the second predicate. This will occur when another comma rule requires us to put a comma in a place that just happens to be before the second predicate.

17.3. I sent a card to my sister, Lisa, and called my brother.

For example, we know the rule to separate non-restrictive appositives with commas (Rule J). Sample 17.3 has the appositive *Lisa*, which is in apposition to *my sister*. Rule J requires us to put commas around *Lisa*. That appositive is just before the second predicate. As a result, we have a comma before the second predicate.

The commas in sample 17.3 are there because of the appositive and not to separate the two predicates. We can check this. If we were to remove the appositive, the comma before the second predicate would also disappear.

At other times, a writer may choose to deliberately break this rule if the first predicate is especially long and complex.

17.4. Explorers hunted for years to find the treasure that the Incas had buried deep in the Andes mountains of Peru many centuries ago, and found it on Tuesday.*

Although this breaks the rules, a writer may choose to do this to help the reader identify the second predicate.

Koan 17

The teacher spoke to the students, saying, "A man rises and walks. What does this tell you?"

Bumbo answered, "A man is his actions."

Bumbo rushed to his desk and started erasing commas.

Explanations of the Koans

Warning: Spoilers ahead!
I recommend that you study the *koans* and try to identify the concepts they illustrate. If you can do that, you will have a greater chance of understanding the concepts, remembering them, and using them in your writing. However, I realize that not everyone learns the same way. I also recognize the possibility that some of these *koans* may be a bit abstract. The *koans* and explanations of the concepts they are intended to illustrate are below.

Koan 1

Bumbo approached his teacher and said, "Teacher, I was taught not to use the comma before the word 'and.' Is that true?" The teacher asked in return, "When did you become a journalist?"

Bumbo is questioning whether or not to use the serial comma, the comma before the conjunction that introduces the final item in a series. If he doesn't use that comma, he will be following the rule from the Associated Press (AP) style guide. The AP style guide is for journalists, so if Bumbo leaves out the serial comma, he will be writing like a journalist.

Koan 2

Bumbo asked his teacher, "Teacher, how can I find the path to correct comma use?" The teacher closed his eyes and said, "Word."

Like many writers, Bumbo is not accustomed to using the serial comma, and he fears that he will forget to do so. When he asks his teacher how he can make sure to use it, his teacher reminds him that the grammar checker in many word processors, such as Microsoft Word, can check for the serial comma automatically.

Koan 3

The teacher went to the platform to give his lesson on commas. He looked at the students, saying nothing. Then he wrote a comma on the wall and left. "Ah," said Bumbo. "Missing words need commas, too!"

When the teacher stands before the students, saying nothing, all his words are implied. What Bumbo learns is that whether the sentence contains all the words or whether some words are purposefully left out, a writer needs to use commas as if they were all there. The comma left behind by the teacher indicates that comma rules apply even when some words are missing from a sentence.

Koan 4

Bumbo asked his teacher, "Do all conjunctions need commas?" The teacher immediately struck him. "Why did you hit me?" Bumbo cried. The teacher answered, "Because."

The word *because* is a conjunction. It is a *subordinating conjunction*, which means it starts a dependent clause. The teacher hits Bumbo to teach him not to put commas in front of all conjunctions, only in front of coordinating conjunctions that join two independent clauses. He answers *because* to indicate that commas before the word *because* is the most common mistake that writers make with putting commas before conjunctions. If you put a comma before *because*, your reader may "hit" you because that comma is wrong.

Koan 5

Bumbo was speaking to a fellow student and said, "Surely, short clauses are not important enough for commas." The teacher walked over to Bumbo, looked up at him, and said, "Who are you to judge?"

Did you notice that the teacher *looked up at him*? The teacher is short or, at least, shorter than Bumbo. Bumbo had just said that short things are not important, and the short teacher was displeased by his attitude. Whether a phrase is short or long, it may confuse the reader. The writer may not be able to judge or predict whether the reader will understand. To increase the potential for reader understanding and avoid the possibility of confusing the reader, the teacher wants Bumbo to use the comma always.

Koan 6

"Have you learned much about commas?" the teacher asked his students. "No teacher," Bumbo wrote in reply. The teacher became sad and said, "Ah, if you use a comma, you will have a teacher."

Look at Bumbo's statement carefully: *No teacher*. He did not use a comma after the word *No*. If he had used a comma, he would have indicated that *No* is an interjection before the name of the person to whom he is responding. However, he left it out, indicating that he did not have a teacher, that he had *no teacher*. A comma would indicate that *No* is an interjection and that *teacher* is the person to whom he is saying *No*.

Koan 7

Bumbo wrote a letter to his parents. At the end of the letter he wrote, "Please give my regards to my sister, Vera." His teacher looked over Bumbo's shoulder and asked, "How many sisters do you have?" Bumbo answered, "Two." "Oh, you wicked student!" his teacher cried. "Your comma just killed one."

The teacher is pointing out how a comma differentiates between a non-restrictive appositive and a restrictive appositive. If the appositive is separated by commas, as in *my sister, Vera*, it is a non-restrictive appositive. This means that the appositive is a perfect one-to-one match with the word to which it is in apposition. In the way Bumbo used the comma, he indicates that *Vera* is a non-restrictive appositive with *my sister*, a perfect one-to-one match. This can only be true if Bumbo has no other sisters. However, Bumbo says he has another sister. Thus, for *Vera* to be a non-restrictive appositive, which is how Bumbo wrote it, the other sister must die.

Koan 8

*Bumbo was interrupted by another student, who also had much to learn about commas. "I met your brother, Bumbo," said the student. "How can that be?" Bumbo asked. "**My** name is Bumbo."*

This koan shows how two comma rules may overlap. In the statement *I met your brother, Bumbo*, the name *Bumbo* (1) might be in apposition to (might have the same meaning as) *your brother*, or (2) might be the name of the person to whom the student is speaking. Is the student claiming that *Bumbo* is the name of *your brother*, or is he directly addressing Bumbo? The problem is that in either case, the name *Bumbo* will be separated by commas. In fact, the student is speaking to Bumbo. Bumbo knows the student is speaking to him, he knows his own name, and he knows the name of his brother, so he should have figured it out. Bumbo is not very smart, and he misinterpreted the statement, thinking the student means his brother's name is Bumbo.

Koan 9

Bumbo approached his teacher with a concerned look on his face. "Teacher," he said, "some commas seem optional. How do I know whether or not to use them?" In response, the teacher asked him, "Two bridges cross the river. One bridge is missing steps, and the other is whole. Which do you use?"

Imagine a pedestrian bridge crossing a river, the

kind with individual boards going across its width. If some of the boards are missing, and if you are not careful about where you walk, you might fall through the bridge. You can cross, but it's risky. On the other hand, a bridge with all the steps will be safe. This is like a sentence with commas. Some commas are required, and some seem optional. However, if some of the commas are missing, the reader might get confused. The teacher wants Bumbo to choose the option that has the greatest chance of helping the reader understand the sentence. This means Bumbo needs to put in all the commas, even the optional ones.

Koan 10

Bumbo and his fellow students were walking to the Temple of Meaning wearing matching robes. They were arguing about who should walk in front. Bumbo called to a passing teacher and asked, "What order should we walk in, teacher?" The teacher answered, "You all look the same to me."

The teacher means that the walking order doesn't matter because they are all alike. They can be in any order, and they will still get to the Temple of Meaning. This is the same as coordinate adjectives. The order doesn't matter. If you put the adjectives in a different order and the sentence has the same meaning, they are coordinate adjectives.

Koan 11

Bumbo stood silently before his teacher, who was writing a lesson about commas. Finally, the teacher looked up from his desk. "It's me, Bumbo," Bumbo said. "I already know which one you are," the teacher answered. "Go stand outside."

The teacher can see Bumbo and knows who is standing before him, but Bumbo tells him anyway. This is unnecessary information, so the teacher sends him away. The teacher wants Bumbo to learn about using commas around non-restrictive phrases. If the reader already knows who or what you are writing about, a description of the person or thing is non-essential and needs to "stand outside" the sentence, meaning it should be separated from it with commas.

Koan 12

A group of tourists were visiting the school, and Bumbo was curious about them. "Teacher," he asked, "may I follow those tourists?" The teacher replied, "Not without a comma."

Bumbo wants to follow behind the tourists, much like a descriptive phrase may follow a sentence. He is not one of them and is not part of their group. He is not connected to them, and they form a complete group whether or not he follows them. Bumbo resembles a descriptive phrase, and the group of tourists resembles a complete sentence. The teacher tells Bumbo that he will need a comma to attach himself to the end of their group in the same way that a descriptive phrase not part of the grammatical structure of the sentence needs a comma in order to follow it.

Koan 13

Bumbo asked, "how can I understand absolute phrases?" His teacher asked in response, "What is the universe?" "It's what is all around us," Bumbo replied, still confused. The teacher nodded sagely and said, "Meditate on the universe, and you will be enlightened."

When Bumbo thinks a bit, he realizes that the universe, by definition, contains everything in it. In that way, the universe defines everything it contains, not just one thing. The teacher wants Bumbo to apply this idea to absolute phrases, which describe everything in the sentence and not just one word. Once Bumbo understands this, he will understand absolute phrases, and he will realize that he needs to separate them with commas to prevent the reader from thinking they are associated with any one part.

Koan 14

Bumbo knocked on the door to the Temple of Meaning and said, "May I come in?" "Did you bring a comma?" his teacher replied. "Yes," Bumbo answered. "Ah," said the teacher, "bring it inside."

Bumbo wants to speak to his teacher, to have a conversation with him. If we write the conversation, the words they speak will be in quotation marks. His teacher, as we have seen, is a stickler for correct comma use, so he reminds Bumbo that they will need commas to separate the quotations from the main sentences. He also knows that the commas go inside the quotation marks. He tells Bumbo to bring the comma inside so that their conversation may be written correctly.

Koan 15

Bumbo wrote a letter to his teacher, stating, "Thank you for teaching me about commas. I now use them as often as possible." When the teacher received the letter, he tore it down the middle and sent the first half back to Bumbo. "Ah," said Bumbo, "not all commas are needed."

Bumbo's letter communicates a complete message. When the teacher tears it in half, top to bottom, each half of the letter only contains part of the message. The first part, which Bumbo receives, needs the second part to communicate the complete message. From this lesson, Bumbo understands that some expressions have two parts. If he separates the second part from the first part by using a comma, the first part will be incomplete and will not communicate the entire message. However, if he leaves out the comma between the two parts, the message will be complete.

Koan 16

Bumbo sat motionless in the Temple of Meaning. His teacher asked what he was doing. "I am learning to use commas," Bumbo told him. "You foolish student," the teacher exclaimed. "If you do not act on what you know, your life will never be complete."

Bumbo, the subject of this *koan*, isn't doing anything. He thinks he is, but he is wrong. The teacher reminds him that a subject without an action is incomplete. He wants Bumbo to learn that a comma should not separate the predicate from the subject because a subject needs a predicate to make a complete sentence.

Koan 17

The teacher spoke to the students, saying, "A man rises and walks. What does this tell you?" Bumbo answered, "A man is his actions." Bumbo rushed to his desk and started erasing commas.

The teacher's sentence illustrates that a man can do more than one action. As Bumbo realizes, a man can do *actions*. In the same way, the subject of the sentence can have more than one predicate. If Bumbo puts a comma before the second predicate, he separates the subject from one of its actions. He already knows that the subject should not be separated from the predicate, so he rushes to find and erase any commas before the second predicate. When he erases those commas, he connects the subject to its actions.

Exercises!

Each of the 34 sentences that follow has only one type of comma error. Some sentences are missing commas, and others have commas in the wrong places. Each chapter on commas is represented by two sentences. The corrected sentences are in the next section.

1. If you read the dictionary, you will learn some new words, your friends will be impressed with your vocabulary and you will become instantly popular at parties.

2. The government is offering subsidies on hybrid cars so I'll think about buying one.

3. Bumbo looked hard for his red pen, his notebook and his shiny shoes, which he had left at home.

4. Bumbo graduated on October 31, 2007 from the Zen Comma School, with the ceremony held in the Temple of Meaning.

5. Yes I can meet you tomorrow at 2:00 after I meet with the clients.

6. Either the air pollution is increasing in urban areas, or municipal water purification systems are becoming aged and ineffective.

7. *300 Days of Better Writing* another book by David Bowman has useful advice about writing clearly.

8. The new bio-fuels which provide lower grade fuel at a higher price are incompatible with many older engine models.

9. The door locked Bumbo had to sleep outside, which is when rain began falling.

10. The symphony began once the sun finally set; however some of the audience members found the late start troublesome and began nodding off before the second movement.

11. The computer hard drive crashed and we lost many important files.

12. Because the weather was cold Bumbo postponed his trip to the beach.

13. After she reached her 90th birthday, her appetite seemed to diminish as was expected.

14. Bumbo left the school when night fell thinking that his teacher had forgotten him.

15. Here are the charts you asked for doctor.

16. The artist's new work comprises beautiful expensive sculptures but reveals his increasing boredom with the media.

17. After the floods receded, the FEMA officers found not only that the city hall had been destroyed by fires caused by submerged electrical wires, but also that the bank had been robbed.

18. Well if you can find the papers I left for you, you will notice that they were submitted on time.

19. After reading this book you will use commas correctly.

Answer Key

The corrected sentences are below, followed by the relevant rule.

(,) = Adds a missing comma.
( ) = Removes a misplaced comma.

1. If you read the dictionary, you will learn some new words, your friends will be impressed with your vocabulary(,) and you will become instantly popular at parties. [Rules A & B]

2. The government is offering subsidies on hybrid cars(,) so I'll think about buying one. [Rule D]

3. Bumbo looked hard for his red pen, his notebook(,) and his shiny shoes, which he had left at home. [Rule A & B]

4. Bumbo graduated on October 31, 2007(,) from the Zen Comma School, with the ceremony held in the Temple of Meaning. [Rule AC]

5. Yes(,) I can meet you tomorrow at 2:00 after I meet with the clients. [Rule I]

6. Either the air pollution is increasing in urban areas ( ) or municipal water purification systems are becoming aged and ineffective. [Rule AG]

7. *300 Days of Better Writing*(,) another book by David Bowman(,) has useful advice about writing clearly. [Rule J]

8. The new bio-fuels(,) which provide lower grade fuel at a higher price(,) are incompatible with many older engine models. [Rule T]

9. The door locked(,) Bumbo had to sleep outside, which is

when rain began falling. [Rule AB]

10. The symphony began once the sun finally set; however(,) some of the audience members found the late start troublesome and began nodding off before the second movement. [Rule N]

11. The computer hard drive crashed(,) and we lost many important files. [Rule D]

12. Because the weather was cold(,) Bumbo postponed his trip to the beach. [Rule G]

13. After she reached her 90th birthday, her appetite seemed to diminish(,) as was expected. [Rule X]

14. Bumbo left the school when night fell(,) thinking that his teacher had forgotten him. [Rule W]

15. Here are the charts you asked for(,) doctor. [Rule M]

16. The artist's new work comprises beautiful(,) expensive sculptures but reveals his increasing boredom with the media. [Rule P]

17. After the floods receded, the FEMA officers found not only that the city hall had been destroyed by fires caused by submerged electrical wires( ) but also that the bank had been robbed. [Rule AG]

18. Well(,) if you can find the papers I left for you, you will notice that they were submitted on time. [Rule I]

19. After reading this book(,) you will use commas correctly. [Rule G]

20. The plaintiff, who lives at 1420 West Wilson Street(,)

Tucumcari(,) New Mexico, hereby declares that the defendant is a liar. [Rule AD]

21. Because our Twitter followers are so nice, we're giving away free books this weekend( ) and providing free cover page editing. [Rule AI]

22. These commercials, disguised as public service announcements, on my favorite radio station( ) seem to repeat endlessly. [Rule AH]

23. Are you aware(,) Bumbo(,) that carpet cleaning solutions may leave a carcinogenic residue? [Rule M]

24. The most important concepts to understand when learning to use commas( ) can be expressed in three words: respect your reader. [Rule AH]

25. "Once upon a time(,)" she began reading aloud. [Rule AG]

26. The cloudy(,) dark sky provided a large gray backdrop to the parade. [Rules P & R]

27. Africanized honey bees(,) we believe(,) are responsible for most bee attacks. [Rule L]

28. However, the rapidly increasing gas prices(,) as you will see(,) are the result of demand, not supply. [Rule L]

29. Bumbo is a student at the Zen Comma School(,) a school established to help people with commas. [Rule J]

30. His training complete, Bumbo was finally able to use commas correctly( ) and communicate his ideas clearly and accurately. [Rule AI]

31. "*Axiom*(,)"( ) she said, "is my favorite word." [Rule AH]

32. The author was pleased with the assistance provided by his editor. Additionally(,) he appreciated the advice that the editor offered on publishing venues. [Rule N]

33. Bumbo wanted to visit with his favorite teacher(,) who was busy correcting exams. [Rule U]

34. Owls(,) unlike bats(,) have exceptional night vision. [Rule AA]

Summary of the Rules

1.   Commas in Series, p. 6
- A.   Separate every item in a series with a comma.
- B.   Use the serial comma.
- C.   Use semicolons to separate items that have their own commas.

2.   Commas when Joining Sentences, p. 10
- D.   Put a comma before a coordinating conjunction that joins two independent clauses.
- E.   Use commas as if implied words were present.
- F.   Don't use a comma before *because* when joining two independent clauses—unless needed by another rule.

3.   Commas after Introductory Descriptions, p. 15
- G.   Put a comma after introductory clauses and phrases.
- H.   Don't separate the descriptive clause or phrase if it occurs at the end of the sentence.

4.   Commas with Interjections, p. 18
- I.   Separate interjections with commas.

5.   Commas with Appositives, p. 20
- J.   Separate non-restrictive appositives with commas.
- K.   Don't use commas to separate restrictive appositives.

6.   Commas with Side Comments, p. 23
- L.   Separate interpolated asides with commas.

7. **Commas with Names, p. 25**

M. When directly addressing someone, place commas around his or her name.

8. **Commas with *Therefore, Too,* and Other Conjunctive Adverbs, p. 26**

N. Separate conjunctive adverbs with commas.

O. Don't use conjunctive adverbs to join independent clauses.

9. **Commas with Adjective Pairs, p. 29**

P. Place a comma between coordinate adjectives.

Q. Leave out the comma between coordinate adjectives to make them non-coordinate and change the meaning.

R. Don't place a comma between non-coordinate adjectives.

S. Don't put a comma between an adjective and the thing it describes.

10. **Commas with *Which* and *Who*, p. 34**

T. Use commas to separate non-restrictive phrases and clauses starting with *which.*

U. Use commas to separate non-restrictive phrases and clauses starting with *who.*

V. Don't use commas to separate restrictive phrases and clauses starting with *who.*

11. **Commas with Final Descriptions, p. 38**

W. Use commas to separate final descriptions that don't refer to the immediately preceding text.

X. Use commas to separate non-grammatical final descriptions.

Y. Use commas to separate final coordinate expressions.

Z. Use a comma to indicate a shift in focus at the end of the sentence.

12. Commas with Parenthetical Expressions and Absolute Phrases, p. 41

AA. Separate parenthetical expressions with commas.

AB. Separate absolute phrases with commas.

13. Commas with Dates, Addresses, Ages, and Titles, p. 44

AC. Put commas around the year when the month and day are included.

AD. Use commas to separate all elements of an address, except the street number and name.

AE. Put commas around ages if they are not part of the grammatical structure.

AF. Put commas around titles if they are not part of the grammatical structure.

14. Commas with Quotations, p. 46

AG. Separate quoted material from the main sentence with commas.

AH. Put the comma inside the final quotation mark.

15. No Commas with *Either…Or* and Other Correlative Pairs, p. 48

AI. Don't separate the two halves of a correlative pair with a comma.

16. No Commas between Subjects and Predicates, p. 50

AJ. Don't use a comma to separate the predicate from the subject.

17. No Commas Between Compound Predicates, p. 52

AK. Don't use a comma to separate two parts of a compound predicate.

More Writing Resources by David Bowman

Visit Hostile Editing (http://hostileediting.com) for more information about these writing resources.

300 Days of Better Writing

300 Top strategies for writing clearly, persuasively, and directly—one strategy at a time presented in plain language. Includes a topic index.

Concise Guide to Technical and Academic Writing

Everything you need to know to produce professional, clear, and credible writing for all types of technical and academic documents. Straightforward instruction for producing great writing.

Bang! Writing with Impact

114 strategies in 18 categories with one purpose: Make your readers pay attention. What the strategies do, how they work, and how to use them successfully.

Precise Edit Training Manual

The 29 most common strategies we use and the problems we fix. Comprehensive, practical instruction on good writing and effective editing.

Which Word Do I Use?

The 26 most commonly mistaken word pairs, fully explained so you can say what you mean.

Writing Tips for a Year

Receive a new writing tip, strategy, resource, or piece of advice—every day for an entire year. That's 365 days of writing instruction delivered by e-mail.

CPSIA information can be obtained
at www.ICGtesting.com
Printed in the USA
LVHW020439310720
661985LV00023B/1245

9 780988 507845